Original title:
The Peaceful Winter Trail

Copyright © 2024 Swan Charm
All rights reserved.

Author: Eliora Lumiste
ISBN HARDBACK: 978-9908-1-1402-6
ISBN PAPERBACK: 978-9908-1-1403-3
ISBN EBOOK: 978-9908-1-1404-0

## The Serenity of Snow-Draped Pines

Snowflakes dance on branches high,
Whispers of joy, as time drifts by.
Softly blanketed, the earth aglow,
Nature's wonder, a peaceful show.

Children laugh in pure delight,
Building memories, spirits bright.
In the stillness, hearts unite,
Under the stars, a silent night.

## A Walk Through Winter's Embrace

Hand in hand, we stroll along,
Breath visible, a joyful song.
Footsteps crunched on powdered white,
In winter's glow, our hearts take flight.

Glistening trees, a sight divine,
With every step, everything aligns.
Chasing shadows, warmth in cheer,
Winter's embrace, we hold so dear.

## Frosted Trails and Whispered Hues

Frosted trails, where we wander free,
Colors twinkling, a vibrant spree.
Paths of silver, whispers of light,
Nature's palette, a pure delight.

Laughter rises, like birds in flight,
Warmth in hearts, on this chilly night.
With every turn, magic unfurls,
A winter's gift, the joy it hurls.

**The Lullaby of Quiet Winters**

In the hush of falling snow,
A lullaby that gently flows.
The world slows down, peace aligns,
Wrapped in warmth beneath the pines.

Candles flicker, hearts aglow,
Stories shared in soft, low tones.
Through the windows, laughter gleams,
Winter's charm, wrapped up in dreams.

**Traces of Peace in the Pale Glow**

In the pale glow, laughter swirls,
Children dance, joy unfurls.
Candles flicker, warm the night,
Traces of peace in soft delight.

Snowflakes drift, a gentle shroud,
Whispers of magic, soft and loud.
Hearts aglow with hopes anew,
In this moment, dreams break through.

Gathered near the crackling fire,
Voices raised, a festive choir.
Echoes of love in every cheer,
Traces of peace, a season dear.

## The Hushed Magic of Winter Wanderings

Wandering through this winter glow,
Magic whispers, soft and low.
Footprints mark the snowy trails,
Hushed delights in frosty gales.

Twinkling lights on every tree,
Nature's charm, a symphony.
Sipping cocoa, warmth bestowed,
In this wonder, hearts explode.

Snowmen rise with cheerful grins,
Joyful laughter, laughter wins.
The night sky sparkles, twinkling bright,
Hushed magic reigns in pure delight.

## Canvas of White Under Starlit Skies

Under starlit skies we roam,
Canvas of white, a winter home.
Magic glimmers in every flow,
As our spirits start to glow.

Winter's breath wraps us tight,
Filling hearts with sheer delight.
Every snowflake tells a tale,
Where love and laughter never pale.

Fires crackle, warmth and mirth,
Celebrating this joyful birth.
In the silence, hear the dreams,
Canvas of white, where wonder beams.

## Stillness Echoing in Frozen Steps

In the stillness, echoes play,
Frozen steps lead the way.
A world adorned in crystal sheen,
Festive hearts in tranquil scenes.

Frosted branches, nature's art,
Whispers of joy filling the heart.
Each moment, a cherished gift,
As spirits and laughter drift.

Gather 'round, ignite the night,
In harmony, the world feels right.
Stillness holding secrets deep,
Echoes of joy, in memories we keep.

## Vows of Solitude in Frozen Time

In the hush of winter's glow,
Sip sweet cocoa, warmth to flow.
Candles flicker, laughter shared,
Promise whispered, hearts prepared.

Snowflakes dance like dreams on air,
Each one unique, none to compare.
Together bound in quiet grace,
In solitude, we find our place.

Fires crackle, stories unfold,
Embarking on journeys bold yet cold.
The world outside, a crystal sheen,
In frozen time, love's evergreen.

With every smile, a vow we make,
In this stillness, we won't forsake.
Winter's breath, a gentle sigh,
In the snow's embrace, we fly high.

## A Journey Through Solitary Stillness

Footsteps crunch on snowy ground,
In silence deep, our hearts are found.
Shadows stretch beneath the trees,
Whispers ride the frosty breeze.

Each breath a cloud, a fleeting sign,
Navigating paths where stars align.
The world is hushed, a sacred pause,
In this beauty, nature's laws.

Wrapped in warmth of woolen knit,
Lost in thoughts, each moment lit.
Frozen lakes reflect the skies,
A journey where stillness lies.

In solitude, reflections gleam,
Every heartbeat, a quiet dream.
Together yet apart we sway,
In winter's peace, we choose to stay.

## **Paths Etched in Ice**

Winding trails beneath the moon,
Stories of ice sing a tune.
Footprints tell of dreams once dreamed,
On paths where light and shadows teamed.

Every crystal sparkles bright,
Casting sparkles in the night.
Shimmering whispers, tales of yore,
Each step opens a frozen door.

The air is thick with frosty cheer,
Every moment, joy draws near.
A ballet of snowflakes swirl,
As nature weaves her quiet pearl.

In quiet halls of winter's reign,
Joy unfurls, negates the pain.
On paths etched in gleaming ice,
Life's simple wonders are so nice.

## **Silent Flight of Winter's Breath**

The world adorned in silent white,
A canvas pure, the day feels right.
With every sigh, the chill unearths,
The magic found in winter's mirth.

Feathered flurries dance and play,
In this moment, dreams find sway.
Breath of frost, a gentle kiss,
In the quiet, find your bliss.

Treetops dressed in glistening lace,
Nature's wonder, a true embrace.
A fleeting glimpse of winter's grace,
A silent flight through this sacred space.

Each whisper of snow is a song,
In the stillness, we both belong.
As night drapes the world, stars ignite,
In winter's heart, everything feels right.

## Trails of Tranquility in Winter

Snowflakes dance with a gleeful twirl,
Children laugh, as their dreams unfurl.
Cozy fires crackle, warmth inside,
Joyous hearts swirling, like the tide.

Blankets of white, a peaceful sight,
Caroling voices bring pure delight.
Hot cocoa steaming, clouds of cream,
In this winter wonderland, we dream.

## Soft Whispers of the Wintry Woods

Crisp air carries soft whispers low,
Pine trees shimmer, in moonlight's glow.
Footprints tracing a path so fine,
Nature's embrace, a sweet design.

Branches adorned in frosty lace,
Echoes of laughter fill the space.
The world is hushed, yet spirits sing,
In the heart of winter, joy takes wing.

## Serene Paths Amongst Frosty Foliage

Glittering paths through frosted leaves,
Golden sunlight, the heart believes.
Nature's canvas, hues intertwined,
A festive wonder, pure and kind.

Gathering friends, stories to share,
Laughter mingles in icy air.
Serenity wrapping each soul tight,
Celebrating warmth through the night.

## Cold Air, Warm Heart

Biting winds that tickle the cheek,
A fiery spirit, adventurous streak.
Cheerful gatherings around the flame,
United in joy, no two hearts the same.

As frost decorates branches so high,
Hope blooms brightly, like stars in the sky.
In the chill of life, we find our part,
Together we stand, cold air, warm heart.

## Moonlit Pathways in the Cold

Beneath the moon, the snowflakes dance,
Light glimmers on each icy chance.
Silent whispers of the night,
As joy ignites with frosty light.

Footprints crunch on pathways white,
Laughter echoes, souls alight.
Warming hearts in chilly air,
Together we embrace the flair.

Twinkling stars above us play,
Guiding dreams on this bright display.
With every step, new stories weave,
In moonlit glow, we dare believe.

Frosty breath like sugar spun,
In this moment, we are one.
Celebrate the world so bright,
On this wondrous, chilly night.

## The Calm Before the Thaw

In quiet shadows, winter waits,
Gentle peace as love creates.
A stillness wraps the land tonight,
In hopes of spring's returning light.

Branches heavy, kissed by snow,
The world inside whispers, slow.
Promises of warmth ahead,
In the silence, dreams are spread.

Crisp the air, with joy we breathe,
As nature holds the magic sheath.
Gathered close, we share our tales,
In cozy nooks, where laughter sails.

The calm before, we cherish now,
With warmth of hearts, we make a vow.
To greet the change, to hold it near,
Together, we'll embrace the cheer.

## Snowy Embrace of Nature

Blankets white on earth bestowed,
A lively dance, the season glowed.
Children laughing, sleds in tow,
In nature's arms, we ebb and flow.

Each snowflake falls, a whisper sweet,
Crafting magic beneath our feet.
Joy in the chill, we run and play,
Wrapped in warmth on winter's day.

Nature beckons with open arms,
With frosted trails and winter charms.
Together we explore the land,
A snowy embrace, perfectly planned.

In this season, bright and bold,
Stories of warmth start to unfold.
With every moment, our spirits rise,
In a snowy world, where wonder lies.

## Wanderings in a Frozen Dream

Through glittering realms our footsteps glide,
In a frozen dream, we take a ride.
Whispers of magic fill the air,
As frosty wonders everywhere.

Wanderlust pulls like a gentle muse,
Inviting us to explore and choose.
In every shadow, a tale untold,
In this land of glimmering gold.

Trees adorned with silvery lace,
We lose ourselves in nature's grace.
Each breath taken, soft and clear,
In this frozen realm, we have no fear.

With each moment, joy is found,
In a world of wonder, so profound.
Let's dance beneath the pale moonlight,
In our frozen dream, we take flight.

## **Tranquil Steps in the Snow**

Footprints crunch underfoot,
Laughter dances in the air,
Children build their snowman,
Joyful echoes everywhere.

Twinkling lights upon the trees,
Fires crackle, warmth to share,
Hot cocoa sipped with glee,
Moments cherished, hearts laid bare.

Scarves wrapped snugly and tight,
Snowflakes twirl, a gentle flight,
Voices blend in soft delight,
Winter's magic, pure and bright.

As we stroll through this wonder,
Memories made, so sweetly spun,
In the chill, our hearts grow fonder,
Underneath the winter sun.

## **Serenity Amongst the Pines**

Whispers of the frosty breeze,
Pine trees sway with gentle grace,
Nature hums its softest pleas,
In this tranquil, tranquil place.

Sunlight filters through the boughs,
Casting shadows on the ground,
Each moment here, a sacred vow,
In serenity, peace is found.

Birds chirp softly from their perch,
Echoing through the snowy glade,
A sense of wonder starts to lurch,
In this stillness, worries fade.

With each breath, the world feels new,
The essence of winter's embrace,
A celebration in every view,
Amongst the pines, a warm space.

**A Still Journey Through Winter**

Frosty air, a diamond sheen,
Snowflakes dance with silent grace,
Every path a silky scene,
Winter's beauty, calm embrace.

Footsteps echo, soft and light,
Crisp and clear beneath the sky,
Stars emerge as day turns night,
Wonders spark as time goes by.

Wrapped in warmth, our laughter flows,
Stories shared by fire's glow,
In this season, love just grows,
Together in the moonlit show.

Through the stillness, joy we find,
Every heartbeat sings anew,
In this journey, hearts entwined,
Winter's magic, pure and true.

## Echoes of Silence in White

Blankets draped on every tree,
Whispered secrets in the night,
The world transforms, a sight to see,
Wrapped in silence, soft and white.

Flickering candles gently sway,
Fireside tales of long ago,
In each breath, the chill gives way,
To warmth, where glowing embers glow.

Snowflakes twirl, a gentle dance,
Every heart beats strong with cheer,
In this moment, take a chance,
To hold each other close and near.

Echoes linger, laughter shared,
In these woods, enchantment grows,
Underneath the starlit glare,
In the quiet, joy just flows.

**Tread Lightly on Winter's Canvas**

Snowflakes dance in the chilly air,
Laughter echoes, joy everywhere.
Carols sung by fireside bright,
Hearts aglow in soft twilight.

Children play in fields of white,
Building dreams in pure delight.
Footprints trail in winding rows,
Magic spreads wherever it goes.

## A Lullaby of the Winter Woods

Whispers of the frosty night,
Stars twinkle with pure delight.
Moonbeams cast a silver hue,
Nature sings a tune so true.

Branches sway with gentle grace,
Nights of wonder, a warm embrace.
Peaceful moments in the snow,
Winter's charm begins to flow.

## Sheltered Beneath Snow-Laden Branches

Glistening flakes on branches rest,
Silent watchers, nature's best.
Underneath, a world serene,
Wrapped in white, a tranquil scene.

Warmth of fires and hearts combined,
Joyful memories intertwined.
Gathered close, the cheer will rise,
Underneath the starlit skies.

**Footfalls of Solitude in the Cold**

Quiet steps on a frosty trail,
Nature's breath, a soothing veil.
Whispers soft in the frozen air,
Each moment, a treasure rare.

Windsong calls through the pines,
A symphony of winter's lines.
Solitude wrapped in purest white,
Finding peace in the starry night.

## Echoes of Stillness Beneath the Boughs

Whispers dance among the leaves,
Joyful laughter fills the air.
Underneath the dappled shade,
Hearts entwined without a care.

Candles twinkle in the night,
Songs of warmth and love ignite.
Underneath the starry skies,
Every moment feels so right.

Gathered close by fireside glow,
Stories shared of long ago.
Time suspended, spirits soar,
Echoes of the night will flow.

As the sun begins to rise,
Joy and laughter, no goodbyes.
Memories of this embrace,
Forever live in heart's reprise.

## A Journey Through Quiet Frost

Chill of night, the world aglow,
Frosty patterns softly show.
Footsteps crunch on wintry ground,
Magic in the silence found.

Candied treats and joyful cheer,
Gathering friends both far and near.
With each smile, the chill grows warm,
In the air, a festive charm.

Branches bare, yet spirit bright,
Underneath the sparkling light.
A journey through this tranquil scene,
Where laughter reigns, and hearts convene.

Beneath the moon's soft silver hue,
Old traditions feel brand new.
As we wander through the frost,
We find the warmth of love, not lost.

## Beneath the Enchanted Canopy

Moonlit nights, the stars align,
Under boughs where magics twine.
Voices rise, a song so sweet,
Dancing in a rhythmic beat.

Flickering lights like fireflies,
Beneath the trees, the laughter flies.
Every heart feels pure delight,
Wrapped in love on this bright night.

Whispers shared in gentle grace,
Memories created in this space.
Underneath the branches wide,
Joy and love will always bide.

As we dream of what's to come,
Warmth of friendship feels like home.
Beneath this enchanted sight,
Our hearts burst with purest light.

## Glistening Paths of Solitude

In twilight's glow, the world is still,
Glistening paths that bend and thrill.
Walking softly through the night,
Stars like lanterns, shining bright.

Solitude holds its gentle sway,
Yet joy awaits in the array.
In this quiet, hearts align,
As laughter mingles, pure divine.

Snowflakes twirl, a soft embrace,
Fleeting moments, time and space.
In the hush, we find our song,
A harmony where we belong.

Down glistening paths, the spirits cheer,
Every heartbeat draws us near.
In solitude, we've come to see,
Together, we are wild and free.

## Unraveled Dreams in White Blankets

Underneath the stars so bright,
Whispers float in frosty night.
Children laughing, hearts aglow,
Wrapped in magic, soft as snow.

Candles flicker, warm and kind,
In this beauty, we unwind.
Chasing dreams on winter's breeze,
Joyful moments, sure to seize.

Mirthful songs on lips do dance,
In the chill, we take a chance.
Sledding down the hills with glee,
Unraveled dreams, wild and free.

As we gather, hand in hand,
Creating memories so grand.
In the glow of love, we trust,
Festive magic, bright and just.

## Respite in the Chilly Caress

Snowflakes twirl, a gentle kiss,
Each one brings a touch of bliss.
Warmth inside, the hearth aglow,
Respite comes in the chilly flow.

Laughter echoes, spirits soar,
Winter's wonder we adore.
Friends and family gathered near,
Filling hearts with festive cheer.

Glistening lights on trees so tall,
Adventurous stories, we recall.
Cocoa sipped in, cozy nights,
Wrapped in warmth and twinkling lights.

Sleds and snowmen mark the days,
In simple joys, our heart plays.
Together, we embrace the chill,
Festive love, a winter thrill.

## **Frost Bitten Yet Unforgotten**

Beneath the stars, the world is still,
Frost-bitten paths, a wondrous thrill.
Memory's echo, soft and sweet,
Fading whispers beneath our feet.

Nature's breath in crystal light,
Wraps us warmly through the night.
Every moment shared anew,
Frosted dreams, forever true.

Carols ringing through the air,
Filling hearts with tender care.
Though the cold may bite and sting,
Joy takes flight on winter's wing.

In every flake, a tale unfolds,
Frost-bitten dreams that warmth holds.
United in this chilly dance,
Festive souls in winter's trance.

## Embracing the Quietude of Winter

Embracing stillness, deep and wide,
Winter whispers, the world aside.
Letting go of all the haste,
In quietude, no time to waste.

Snowy blankets cover ground,
Softest silence all around.
In this pause, we find our peace,
From the chaos, sweet release.

Fires crackle, warmth does swell,
In this calm, we weave our spell.
Mug in hand, stories to share,
Together, hearts laid bare.

Performing dances in the snow,
Festive spirits start to glow.
In the quietude we trust,
Winter's embrace, bright and just.

**Gentle Footprints on Ice**

Glistening paths where laughter rings,
Children dance, their joy takes wing.
Soft whispers echo on the breeze,
Moments captured, hearts at ease.

Sparkling crystals twinkle bright,
Underneath the pale moonlight.
Sleds and shouts fill the air,
Festive spirits everywhere.

Ribbons tied with bows of cheer,
Warmth and smiles, loved ones near.
Hot cocoa steaming in hand,
Together we joyfully stand.

Gentle laughter weaves a song,
Celebrations all night long.
These prints in ice, a cherished trace,
Of treasured moments, a joyful place.

# **Melodies of the Quiet Woods**

Hushed tones drift through trees so grand,
   Whispers of magic across the land.
Crunching leaves beneath our feet,
   Nature's rhythm, soft and sweet.

Birds take flight with tunes so clear,
   Symphonies for all to hear.
Sunshine dapples through the green,
   A festive touch, a tranquil scene.

Frolicking deer skip with grace,
In this enchanting, lovely space.
Friends gather, stories shared,
Memories made, showing we care.

Every breeze brings joy anew,
In twilight's glow, a vibrant hue.
Nature's concert, warm and bright,
   Such sweet melodies, pure delight.

**Frost-Kissed Forest Adventures**

A world transformed in icy glow,
Frosted trees in rows, they show.
Glimmers dance on every branch,
In winter's wonderland, we prance.

Tracks of critters mark the snow,
Every turn, a new tableau.
Laughter echoes through the pines,
Adventure calls in joyful signs.

Bundled close, we brave the chill,
With hearts so warm, we climb the hill.
Slides and rolls, our spirits rise,
Underneath these sparkling skies.

Sharing stories by the fire's glow,
In this haven, time moves slow.
The frosty air, a joyful kiss,
Moments like these, we won't miss.

## Hushed Harmony Amidst Snowflakes

Snowflakes fall like gentle dreams,
Whispers of winter's softest themes.
Glistening landscapes all around,
In this silence, joy is found.

Laughter mingles in the air,
Unity in moments we share.
As twilight casts a golden hue,
On this canvas, friendships brew.

Hearts aglow with warmth and cheer,
Every glance, a bond sincere.
Stars above, a twinkling crown,
In this peace, we never frown.

Together we embrace the night,
With love that sparkles, pure and bright.
Snowflakes dance, as we rejoice,
In this hush, we find our voice.

## **Beneath the Snow**

Laughter dances in the air,
Children bundle, without a care.
Bright lights twinkle all around,
Joyful hearts in every sound.

Mittens clash in snowy play,
Dreams unfold in winter's sway.
Hot cocoa warms our glowing night,
Under stars, our spirits light.

## Seeds of Rest

Whispers soft as twilight falls,
In every nook, the laughter calls.
Gifts wrapped in glittering cheer,
Gathering close, we bring the year.

Merry moments, tales to share,
As winter's breath fills the air.
Hopeful wishes take their flight,
In the quiet of the night.

## The Grasp of Winter's Silence

In stillness deep, the world appears,
A canvas white, no hint of fears.
Beneath the moon's soft glow so bright,
Dreams unfurl in quiet light.

Footprints whisper on the snow,
Each step marks where friendships grow.
Together here, in calm we bind,
The grasp of peace, with warmth entwined.

## Resolutions Found in Frosted Landscapes

Amidst the frost, new dreams arise,
Beneath the cold, warm hopes surprise.
With every breath, fresh goals ignite,
Woven in the starlit night.

Gathered close, we take a stand,
Embrace the change, heart in hand.
In playful snow, our spirits soar,
Resolutions that we adore.

**Gentle Echoes in a White Wonderland**

Softly glows the evening's charm,
Each heartbeat wrapped in winter's arm.
Echoes of laughter fill the space,
In this wondrous, frozen place.

Underneath the silver skies,
Magic dances in our eyes.
Together here, the world feels bright,
In this gentle, tender night.

## Layers of Peace in the Winter's Hold

Snow blankets softly, a gentle embrace,
Children are laughing, joy fills the space.
Lights shine like stars in the night's deep blue,
Warm hearts unite, as the cold wind blew.

Fires crackle softly, stories unfold,
Moments to cherish, memories bold.
Mug of hot cocoa, steam rising high,
Under winter's spell, the long hours fly.

## Secrets of the Frosted Grove

Whispers of nature, in silence they wait,
Trees draped in snow, a magical fate.
Footprints are lost in the glittering white,
Mysteries linger in the soft moonlight.

Branches like whispers, so delicate, light,
Hidden in wonder, pure nature's delight.
Birds in their nests, all cuddled with care,
Secrets of winter enchant in the air.

## Under the Weight of Winter's Hand


Clouds hang like curtains, draping the sky,
Each flake a dancer, as they twirl and fly.
Frozen stillness fills the woods all around,
A world wrapped in silence, so peaceful, profound.

The earth wears a robe of crystalline glow,
Nature's own artwork, as gentle winds blow.
Children in snowballs, laughter and cheer,
Under winter's hand, love draws us near.

## A Celestial Dance of Snowflakes

Snowflakes are twirling, a ballet divine,
Each one unique, like a shimmering sign.
They waltz through the air, so light and so free,
A celestial dance, for all eyes to see.

Guiding the night with their silent parade,
Frosted confetti in a grand masquerade.
Moonlight reflecting on crystals aglow,
In this festive wonder, our spirits will grow.

## The Gentle Touch of Icy Breath

In the winter's soft embrace,
Laughter echoes, pure and bright,
Snowflakes dance in merry chase,
Twinkling stars adorn the night.

Hot cocoa warms our chilly hands,
Children play in fields of white,
Joyous songs from merry bands,
Hearts alight with sheer delight.

Lanterns glow with amber light,
Fires crackle, spirits soar,
Friends gather, hearts unite,
Creating memories to adore.

As the icy breath whispers near,
Hope and cheer intertwine,
In this festive time of year,
Love and laughter brightly shine.

## A Voyage Through Winter's Embrace

On a sled we coast and glide,
Through the snow, our laughter flies,
Magical whispers by our side,
Underneath vast, starlit skies.

Frosty air fills our lungs bright,
Sparks of joy in every heart,
Chasing dreams through the cold night,
Winter's stage, a wondrous art.

Bonfires crackle, warmth resides,
Stories shared, our spirits sing,
Along this path, the joy collides,
In every moment, love takes wing.

Beneath the moon's enchanting glow,
We celebrate each precious cheer,
In this dance, our spirits flow,
This winter's embrace, dear and near.

## **Moments Frozen in Time**

Icicles shimmer, a crystal show,
Captured beauty, a fleeting glance,
In this winter, soft winds blow,
Time stands still in a joyful dance.

Fleeting moments, laughter bright,
Frosty breaths against the air,
Memories made in the purest light,
Whispers echo, love laid bare.

Every snowflake falls anew,
A unique story it will tell,
In this wonderland of view,
Moments frozen, we know well.

Gather round the fire's glow,
Share your dreams, let spirits rise,
In this festive ebb and flow,
Time is magic in disguise.

## **Whispers of the Frosted Path**

Through the woods, softly we tread,
Frosty whispers call in the night,
Each step taken, paths we've led,
In winter's arms, we find delight.

Branches draped in silvery lace,
Nature's beauty, pure and rare,
In this tranquil, magical place,
Every heartbeat, love to share.

Candles flicker, shadows play,
Songs of joy fill the crisp air,
Together we'll laugh and sway,
Creating bonds beyond compare.

Embrace the joy, let spirits lift,
As we dance down this frosted trail,
In every moment, find the gift,
In winter's wonder, we prevail.

## **The Frosty Kiss of Wandering Spirits**

In winter's embrace, where snowflakes dance,
Joyful whispers beckon, a merry romance.
Laughter echoes softly beneath the moon's glow,
Frosty kisses linger, as spirits bestow.

Chasing the twilight, with heartbeats in sync,
Crisp air fills the night, causing dreams to think.
Wanderers gather, with stories to share,
In a chilly wonderland, magic fills the air.

Fireside tales spark, igniting the night,
Roasting sweet treats that are pure delight.
With arms open wide, we embrace the cheer,
In this frosty realm, we hold loved ones near.

So, raise a glass high, to the joy we create,
For wandering spirits, we celebrate fate.
The frost gently kisses our hearts in delight,
Embracing the magic that glimmers in white.

## Habitual Peace in the Cold

Beneath frosted branches, the world feels all right,
Whispers of peace swirl in the soft, starry night.
With each twinkling light, our worries take flight,
In quietude nestled, our hearts reunite.

Snowflakes keep falling, a soft lullaby,
Carving a canvas, the stillness nearby.
Together we gather, with spirits so bright,
In habitual peace, bathed in silver light.

The glow of the lanterns paints shadows that play,
As laughter and love wrap the chilly decay.
Each moment a treasure, a bond to uphold,
In this tranquil embrace, true warmth we behold.

So, let's toast to journeys that weave through the air,
To warmth found in friendship, a joy we all share.
In the heart of the cold, our spirits take hold,
In habitual peace, let the magic unfold.

## The Warmth Within the Chill

In the frostbitten air, smiles brightly bloom,
Even the coldest nights can't seal warmth in gloom.
We gather around fires, hearts open wide,
Embracing the magic, our worries aside.

The world may be frozen, but love finds a way,
Through chilly adventures, we savor the day.
Hand in hand we wander, through snowflakes we glide,
With warmth within us, there's nothing to hide.

The laughter of children, like bells in the night,
Threads of togetherness wrapped in pure light.
Each moment a treasure, a dance full of grace,
In the warmth within chill, we find our own place.

So, let's sing of the joy that our hearts intertwine,
Through the coldest of nights, our spirits will shine.
In this festive embrace, let each dream fulfill,
For love is the warmth that resides in the chill.

## Crystalline Wilderness Awaits

Enter the wild, where the crystals gleam bright,
Nature's own twinkling, a pure, starry sight.
With each crunch of snow, our spirits take flight,
In crystalline wilderness, adventure ignites.

The trees wear their silver, a frosty attire,
Sparkling in sunlight, they never tire.
Gathering together, we breathe in the thrill,
In the heart of the woods, our laughter will fill.

From hilltops we tumble, down slopes we slide,
In the joy of this moment, we play, we glide.
Snowflakes are falling like dreams from above,
In crystalline wonder, we celebrate love.

So come, take my hand, let's dance in the glow,
In the wilderness waiting, a soft, gentle snow.
For magic's alive; it's the joy that creates,
In the crystalline wilderness, our heart captivates.

## Gentle Glades in Shimmering White

In glades so gentle, crisp and bright,
The snowflakes dance in winter's light.
Trees wear their coats of purest white,
While whispers float through the starry night.

Laughter rings from children near,
With joyful hearts and endless cheer.
Snowmen rise, a frosty cheer,
As festive spirits draw us near.

Fires crackle, warmth invites,
Families gather, hearts ignite.
Stories shared through chilly nights,
In shimmering glades, pure delight.

So let us savor this snowy scene,
In gentle glades, where all is serene.
A festival of nature's grace,
In glistening white, a warm embrace.

## The Winter's Breath of Restful Moments

Breath of winter, soft and sweet,
A blanket white, beneath our feet.
Moments rest in frosted air,
As time suspends without a care.

Candles flicker, shadows play,
In quietude of this holiday.
A tranquil hush blankets the land,
Each peaceful breath, a gentle hand.

Hot cocoa warms our chilly palms,
With spicy scents and cozy balms.
Laughter lingers, hearts embrace,
In this restful, joyful space.

A time to pause, reflect, and dream,
In winter's breath, let spirits beam.
For in these moments, true delight,
Awaits us all, in soft twilight.

## A Symphony in Silence and Snow


In silent fields where snowflakes fall,
A symphony plays, enchanting all.
The world adorned in hushed refrain,
As dreams emerge from winter's lane.

Each flake a note, a gentle sound,
In nature's song, we all are found.
Soft whispers glide on frosty air,
A melody of peace to share.

Beneath the stars, we watch and wait,
For joy and love to emulate.
In moonlit glow, the night is bright,
Composing tunes of pure delight.

Together we shall sing along,
In harmony, we all belong.
For in this symphony of snow,
Our hearts will dance, our spirits glow.

## Shadows of Serenity in the Woods

In woods adorned with frosty lace,
Serenity finds its quiet place.
Shadows linger, softly weave,
In gentle whispers, hearts believe.

The paths are lined with glimmering light,
A tranquil walk, so pure and bright.
Amid the trees, a world of calm,
Where every breath feels like a balm.

Footprints trace through shimmering snow,
As nature's blessings gently flow.
In solitude, we find our way,
Through shadowed woods where dreams can sway.

So let us wander, find the peace,
In winter's hold, our worries cease.
In shadows deep, together stand,
In serene woods, hand in hand.

## Reflections in the Crystal Snow

Sparkling flakes dance in the light,
As joy and laughter fill the night.
Children's voices echo in play,
In winter's embrace, we celebrate the day.

Twinkling lights adorn every tree,
A magical sight, so wild and free.
With mugs of cocoa, warm and sweet,
We gather 'round for festive treats.

Each footprint tells a tale of cheer,
As we share stories held so dear.
Reflections of love in the glistening white,
In the heart of winter, everything feels right.

## The Beauty of a Silent Stroll

With every step, the world slows down,
In the hush of snow, no need for a frown.
Whispers of winter, soft and clear,
Nature wraps us in a cloak of cheer.

The trees wear diamonds, so pristine,
A canvas of white, a tranquil scene.
Lost in the beauty of frosted nights,
Where even the stars shine with pure delight.

Footprints shared, side by side,
In the beauty of silence, our hearts collide.
Each moment cherished, a gift to hold,
In winter's embrace, our stories unfold.

## Chasing Peace Through the Blizzards

In swirling winds, we find our way,
Chasing the peace of a winter's day.
The world draped in a soft, white veil,
Every flake dancing, telling a tale.

Hearts gather warmth in a cozy nook,
With tales of adventure from every book.
We sink in laughter, as snowflakes drift,
In the chill of the night, we share this gift.

Blizzard's fury brings us near,
In each other's company, there's nothing to fear.
Together we conquer the frosty air,
In a season of wonder, love is everywhere.

## The Allure of a Frosty Morning

Morning light glimmers on icy streams,
Awakening wishes, igniting dreams.
Frost-kissed air, so bold and bright,
Invites us outside, to bask in the light.

Snowflakes twirl like delicate lace,
Each moment savored, a joyful embrace.
With laughter ringing through chilly air,
The allure of winter, beyond compare.

Hot drinks in hand, we stroll with glee,
The world transformed, it's pure jubilee.
In the magic of frost, our spirits soar,
Each morning a treasure, we can't ignore.

## Hushed Moments on the Frosty Path

Footprints whisper on the snow,
A gentle chill begins to blow.
Laughter echoes through the trees,
As joy dances with the breeze.

Twinkling lights adorn the night,
Hearts aglow, spirits bright.
Warmth surrounds the frosty air,
In this moment, we all share.

Bundled close, we stroll in mirth,
Each step is filled with playful worth.
The world transformed, so pure and white,
Gathered here, all feels just right.

Hot cocoa warms our hands with cheer,
In the stillness, love draws near.
Let's linger longer, forget the race,
In these hushed moments, find our place.

## Serenity in Each Snowflake's Dance

Falling softly, snowflakes fall,
Nature's magic wrapping all.
Whirls and twirls in the cold embrace,
Each one brings a smile to face.

Children laugh, their cheeks aglow,
Building dreams in mounds of snow.
A flurry of joy, a playful sight,
As day melts into serene night.

Pine trees dressed in frosted white,
Stand like sentinels of the night.
Whispers of winter, calm and clear,
In this dance, we hold each dear.

Bonfires crackle, songs arise,
Beneath the starry winter skies.
With every flake, we find romance,
In the serenity of winter's dance.

## **Quietude Wrapped in White**

Blankets of snow cloak the earth,
A peaceful hush, a moment's worth.
Crackling fires, the scent of pine,
In cozy corners, spirits shine.

Softly falling, a world divine,
As we gather, hearts entwine.
Sparkling lights adorn the scene,
Creating dreams so calm and serene.

Snowmen smile with button eyes,
Underneath the starlit skies.
With each gentle flake we gain,
A quietude that breaks the strain.

Together, we share this space,
Wrapped in warmth, love's sweet embrace.
In this white world, pure and bright,
Let us cherish this peaceful night.

## A Symphony of Snow and Silence

Listen closely, a soft refrain,
Nature hums a soft domain.
Snow-covered hills, a canvas wide,
In silence, let our hearts reside.

Melodies of joy float in the air,
Frosty breezes whisper a prayer.
Every flake a note in time,
Creating rhythms, oh so sublime.

As families gather, laughter flows,
Hot fires crackle, warmth bestows.
In this symphony, love's embrace,
We find our solace, our rightful place.

Under stars, the world aglow,
Together, we create the show.
In harmony with snow and light,
We dance through this enchanted night.

## Whispers of Tranquility in Snowy Pines

The pines are draped in white,
A gentle hush fills the night.
Stars twinkle with soft delight,
In dreams of peace, we take flight.

Snowflakes dance on winter's breath,
With every whisper, a new depth.
Nature's warmth, a quiet myth,
In tranquil woods, we find our heft.

Fires crackle, laughter glows,
As friendship blooms, the warmth flows.
Memories linger, and love grows,
Filling our hearts with sweet prose.

Underneath the moon's soft gaze,
Time stands still in a gentle haze.
We bask in joy, in simple ways,
Creating magic on winter days.

## Gliding Through the Silver Stillness

Gliding softly, crisp and clear,
In silver stillness, we draw near.
Each whispering breeze, we hear,
Welcoming the festive cheer.

Trees cloaked in a frosty glow,
The world is wrapped in pure white snow.
Together, moving slow and low,
With every laugh, our spirits flow.

Footprints marked upon the ground,
Joyful echoes all around.
Nature's silence, a sacred sound,
In winter's arms, our hearts are found.

As we glide through this wonderland,
Hand in hand, we understand.
Peace and love, a gentle strand,
In this snowy realm so grand.

## Calm Waters of the Winter Trail

By calm waters, reflections gleam,
Winter's beauty, a crystal dream.
Tranquil paths where spirits beam,
Beneath the sunlight's warm theme.

The air is crisp, a soothing balm,
Nature whispers, pure and calm.
In the distance, a gentle psalm,
Each moment shared, a sacred charm.

We wander through the frosty glade,
Every step, a memory made.
In laughter's echo, warm and staid,
A tapestry of joy displayed.

With friends around the fire's light,
Fables spun throughout the night.
In quiet moments, hearts unite,
Beneath the stars, our dreams take flight.

## Shadows and Light in a Winter Wonderland

In a wonderland, shadows play,
With flickering lights that find their way.
Dancing snowflakes, bright and gay,
A festive spirit in the fray.

Beneath the boughs, whispers abound,
In laughter's echo, warmth is found.
Magic stirs in every sound,
As winter wraps the world around.

With joyful hearts, we sing and sway,
Chasing twilight into day.
Together, love is here to stay,
In shadows and light, we find our way.

Fires crackle and stories unfold,
With every moment, memories gold.
In this wonderland, hearts so bold,
We treasure warmth against the cold.

## Where the Chill Kisses the Ground

Snowflakes dance across the air,
Laughter echoes, everywhere.
Warm hearts glow in frosty light,
Joyful spirits take their flight.

Children build a castle grand,
With tiny snowballs in their hand.
Scarves wrapped tight, cheeks aglow,
In this wonderland, we flow.

Candles flicker, shadows play,
As twilight welcomes the close of day.
Friends gather 'round with stories shared,
The chill of night, we've often dared.

Hot cocoa warms, as smiles bloom,
Fires crackle, dispelling gloom.
Where the chill kisses the ground,
A festive joy in us is found.

## The Calm Embrace of Winter's Breath

Gentle whispers of the snow,
A tranquil night, soft lights aglow.
Frosty windows, patterns lace,
A calm embrace, a quiet space.

Stars above, like diamonds shine,
In this moment, all is fine.
Families gather, stories flow,
Winter's breath, a soothing glow.

Outside, the world is still and bright,
In cozy homes, hearts feel the light.
With every laugh, our worries cease,
In winter's arms, we find our peace.

The warmth of love, a cherished gift,
In the chilly air, our spirits lift.
The calm embrace of winter's breath,
A joyful dance that knows no death.

## Nature's Quilt of Soft Serenity

A blanket white on every tree,
Nature's quilt, wild and free.
Soft silence falls, the world at rest,
In this wonder, we are blessed.

Footprints lead to hidden nooks,
Underneath the ancient oaks.
Children giggle, angels' flight,
In the hush of soft twilight.

Frosted pine and berry red,
Joy ignites where hearts are fed.
Through the woods, we roam and play,
In nature's quilt, we find our way.

Echoes of laughter fill the air,
Magic lives in our shared care.
Nature's quilt of soft serenity,
Wraps us in its warm infinity.

## Crystal Dreams in a Frozen Landscape

A winter's night wrapped in dreams,
Crystal lights and gentle beams.
Underneath the starry glow,
A frozen world begins to show.

Skaters glide on glistening ice,
In this realm, we pay the price.
With every twirl, our spirits rise,
In crystal dreams beneath the skies.

Hot apple cider warms our hands,
As laughter fills the wooded lands.
With every cheer, we outshine dark,
In this frozen world, we leave our mark.

From frosty breath, true magic flows,
In winter's beauty, love only grows.
Crystal dreams in a frozen landscape,
Together, every heart will escape.

## **Nature's Breath on a Chilly Day**

Upon the frost-kissed earth we tread,
Sprightly whispers dance, joy widespread.
A symphony of crunch underfoot,
Nature's breath wraps us, snug and cute.

Glimmers of sunlight break through the grey,
Warming the hearts in a festive display.
Children's laughter revives the air,
Creating memories beyond compare.

Trees wear their coats of sparkling white,
Each branch adorned, a pure delight.
The sky, a canvas of cobalt blue,
Inviting our spirits to start anew.

As evening falls with a twinkling glow,
The world transforms in a magical show.
Together we gather, hand in hand,
In nature's embrace, a joyful band.

## Finding Solace in Winter's Grasp

In the hush of winter, calm prevails,
Soft snowflakes glide, the world exhales.
A heartwarming fire crackles bright,
Gathered close on this chilly night.

The chill in the air sparking delight,
With hot cocoa warming hands so tight.
Storytelling under blankets warm,
Our laughter, a shelter from the storm.

Outside the frost paints whimsical scenes,
Creating a tapestry of evergreen dreams.
Icicles gleam in the soft moon's gaze,
Casting shadows that dance and sway.

In this hush, we find our peace,
Every moment, a tender fleece.
Together we nestle, love's embrace,
Finding solace in winter's grace.

## Tales Told by Icicle Gleams

Icicles hang like crystal spears,
Whispering tales of winter's cheers.
Glisten and sparkle in the morn's light,
A wondrous display, a sparkling sight.

Daylight dances on frosty eaves,
Nature's magic, a web that weaves.
Underneath skies of gleaming blue,
Stories unfold, each moment is new.

The air is crisp, a festive sign,
With laughter echoing, hearts entwine.
Children chase snowflakes, find their joy,
Nature's own wonderland to employ.

Each icicle sings as the sun departs,
Wrapping the world in its gentle arts.
With warmth in our hearts, we gather near,
Tales told by gleams, festive and clear.

## **Stillness Beneath a White Veil**

A blanket of snow, so soft and white,
Covers the world in a tranquil light.
Footprints lead on to paths unknown,
In this frosty stillness, love has grown.

The trees stand tall, like sentinels dear,
Guarding the whispers of winter's cheer.
With every gust, the silence breaks,
Breathless moments that the heart wakes.

Candlelit windows glow from within,
Inviting warmth as the night begins.
Gathering close, the stories ignite,
Stillness wraps us, cozy and bright.

As stars twinkle in the expansive night,
Every heartbeat feels just right.
Under the veil, together we stay,
In festive prayer as night turns to day.

## **Snow-Blanketed Whispers**

Softly falls the snow at night,
A blanketed world, pure and white.
Laughter dances on the breeze,
Whispers of joy 'neath frosted trees.

The twinkling lights in windows glow,
As carolers sing of love and snow.
Children build, their smiles aglow,
In this festive realm where hearts overflow.

## Serene Steps Through Crystal Woods

Through crystal woods, our laughter flows,
With every step, the holiday grows.
Branches shimmer with icy lace,
Nature's magic, a warm embrace.

The crunch of snow beneath our feet,
In this serene, enchanted retreat.
We gather round with friends so dear,
In festive spirits, we spread good cheer.

## Frosty Reverie Under Moonlit Skies

Under the moon, in frosty night,
Stars twinkle down, a wondrous sight.
We gather close, with tales to tell,
In frosty reverie, all is well.

The chill in air feels warm with love,
As whispers mingle with the stars above.
Toasting to joy, with hearts aligned,
In this magic, true peace we find.

## Tranquil Footprints in Silent Snow

Tranquil footprints mark the way,
In silent snow where children play.
Each step a memory, soft and bright,
In the silence of this winter night.

A gentle breeze sings songs of yore,
As families gather, sharing more.
Festive wishes on the air,
Amidst the snowflakes, love we share.

# **Frosted Memories of Yesteryears**

In twilight glow, the laughter sings,
Footsteps soft on frosty cling.
Bundled up in scarlet scarves,
Each whisper of joy, the heart starves.

Nostalgic lights on branches gleam,
The warmth of friends, a cherished dream.
Winter tales by fireside shared,
With every moment, love declared.

Hot cocoa swirls, a sweet delight,
Sparkles dance in the sparkling night.
Memories wrapped in silver threads,
As we recount what friendship spreads.

In this frosted realm we find,
The joy of past and future aligned.
With every breath, the magic stays,
In frosted memories, sunlight rays.

## Surrendering to Winter's Embrace

Snowflakes twirl in a gentle dance,
Whispering secrets, a quiet romance.
Blankets of white on the world unfold,
Surrendering hearts to the winter cold.

Hushed tranquility fills the air,
Frosty kisses, a moment rare.
Dreams weave softly, like stars above,
Nestled in layers of warmth and love.

Each breath is a cloud, a fleeting sight,
In winter's embrace, our souls alight.
Glistening branches, a silent choir,
Rustling softly, a soothing fire.

With every flake, we choose to hide,
In winter's heart, where we abide.
Through snowy scenes, our spirits soar,
In surrender, we find so much more.

## **Enchanted Trails Beneath a Silver Sky**

Under the glow of a silver beam,
Nature sings in a perfect theme.
Footprints trail on paths anew,
Where every step brings magic too.

Laughter echoes, the joy runs free,
In enchanted woods, just you and me.
Snowflakes drift on the woodland floor,
Each fluttering dance, we can't ignore.

Crisp air brims with delightful mirth,
As we explore this winter's hearth.
Winding trails lead to wonders bright,
In the embrace of a starry night.

With every twist, our hearts ignite,
Beneath the sky, so pure, so bright.
In this magic, we wander and roam,
Finding the path that leads us home.

## Meditations in the Snow's Embrace

In tranquil moments, softly laid,
The snowflakes dance, a gentle parade.
Thoughts drift like clouds, serene and slow,
In the stillness, we come to know.

Embraced by chill, we find our peace,
Nature's rhythm, a sweet release.
In silence deep, the world transforms,
As every flake, a new heart warms.

Muffled sounds and laughter blend,
In these moments, our hearts mend.
Joyful echoes in the crisp air,
With every breath, we strip despair.

Together in this snowy place,
Meditations in winter's grace.
Connecting hearts with hopes aligned,
In the snow's embrace, true peace we find.

## **Voices of the Wind on a Snowy Trail**

Whispers of joy in the frosty air,
Laughter and song, they dance everywhere.
Snowflakes twirl, like dreams set free,
In the heart of winter, we find our glee.

Footprints in white, a story we weave,
Moments of magic, on this eve.
Voices of nature, in harmony blend,
On this snowy trail, where warmth transcends.

Stars appear, like diamonds in the night,
Guiding our spirits, with soft, gentle light.
Each breath taken, a cloud of delight,
Voices of the wind, our hearts ignite.

Gathered together, in joy we share,
Memories crafted, with love and care.
On this snowy trail, let laughter rise,
Voices of the wind, beneath winter skies.

# Flickers of Light in Midwinter Calm

Twirling flames dance in the quiet night,
Warmth in our hearts, a comforting sight.
Flickers of joy, like stars they gleam,
In midwinter calm, we live the dream.

Shadows sway softly, in rhythm they play,
Moments of peace guide us on our way.
Candles aglow, their whispers so bright,
Flickers of wonder in the depths of night.

Snowflakes surround us, a delicate lace,
Each flake unique, like a warm embrace.
In this serene spell, we find our cheer,
Flickers of light, draw loved ones near.

A gathering of souls, in laughter we trust,
In the warmth of the glow, our spirits combust.
Flickers of joy that break the cold's might,
In midwinter calm, we shine so bright.

# Lake of Tranquil Reflections

Beneath the soft glow of the silver moon,
A lake lies still, like a whispered tune.
Tranquility dances on waters so clear,
Reflections of joy, in this haven dear.

Ripples of laughter spread wide and free,
As friends gather close, sharing their glee.
Nature's own mirror, of harmony made,
In the lake's embrace, all worries fade.

Golden sunrises paint skies anew,
In the heart of the lake, dreams break through.
Moments of stillness, beneath trees so grand,
The beauty we cherish, as life's gentle hand.

Laughter resounds, in the cool morning air,
At the lake of tranquil reflections, we share.
With every soft breeze, our spirits arise,
In nature's embrace, we find our skies.

## **Hibernating Earth in Stillness**

Wrapped in a blanket of soft, pure snow,
The earth takes a pause, its energy low.
Hibernating heart, resting so deep,
In stillness it whispers, secrets to keep.

Frosted branches glimmer, a sparkling sight,
While shadows dance softly, in the pale light.
Nature prepares for the springtime's sweet song,
In hibernating earth, where we all belong.

Chill in the air, but warmth in our souls,
Gathered together, we make ourselves whole.
Stories we share by the crackling fire,
In hibernating earth, our spirits inspire.

As seasons will change, and time marches on,
In stillness we find love, a beautiful dawn.
Hibernating earth, with secrets to tell,
In the embrace of winter, all is well.

www.ingramcontent.com/pod-product-compliance
Ingram Content Group UK Ltd.
Pitfield, Milton Keynes, MK11 3LW, UK
UKHW022114211224
452733UK00012B/602

9 789908 114033